To:

_____

From:

_____

Date:

_____

Published by Christian Art Publishers
PO Box 1599, Vereeniging, 1930, RSA

© 2018
First edition 2018

Designed by Christian Art Publishers

Images used under license from Shutterstock.com

Printed in China

ISBN 978-1-4321-2732-9

18 19 20 21 22 23 24 25 26 27 – 11 10 9 8 7 6 5 4 3 2

FAITH
Hope
Love

LIVE A LIFE OF Love

EPHESIANS 5:2

GIVE thanks to the Lord for His UNFAILING LOVE.

Psalm 107:31

By
grace
you have
been saved
through faith,
& that not of yourselves;
it is the
gift of god.

EPHESIANS 2:8

As we Live in God, our LOVE grows more perfect.

1 John 4:17

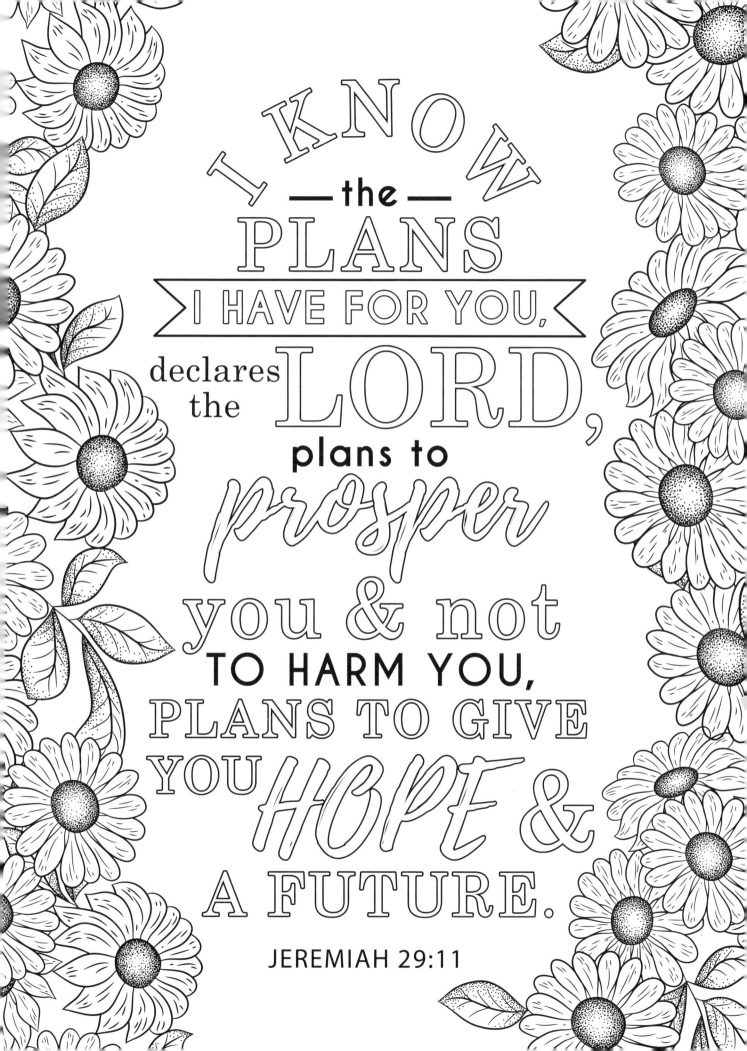

Love...

always protects,
always trusts,
always hopes,
always perseveres.

1 Corinthians 13:7

BE JOYFUL IN *hope,* PATIENT IN AFFLICTION, *faithful* IN PRAYER.
ROMANS 12:12

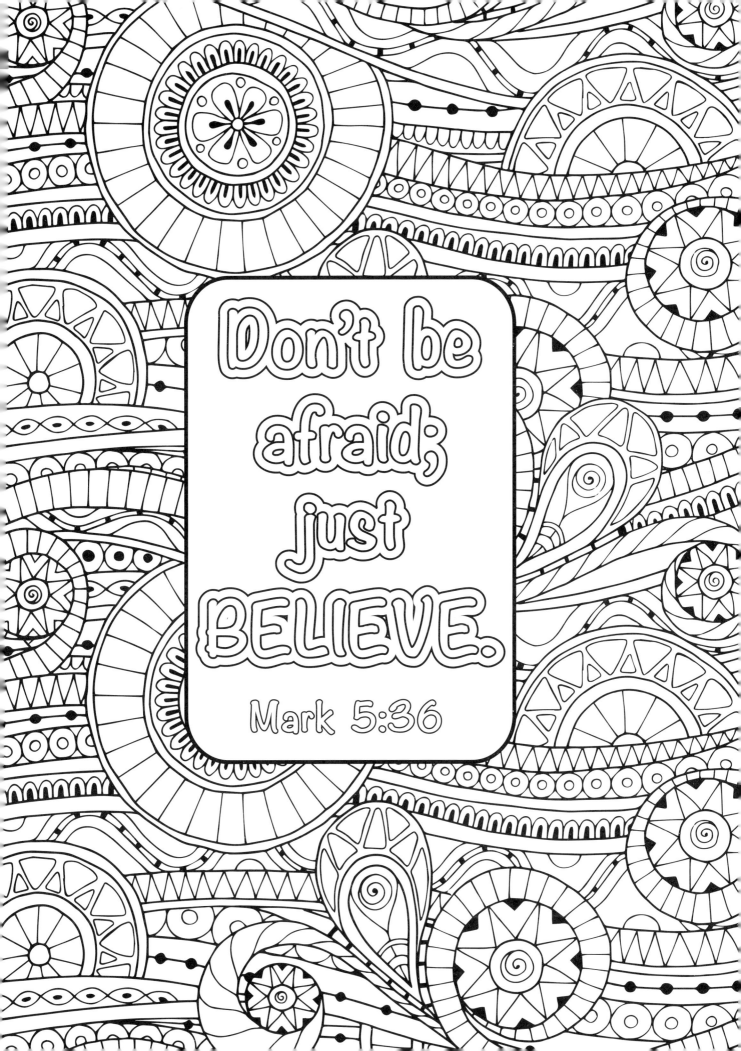

We LIVE by faith, not by SIGHT.

2 Corinthians 5:7

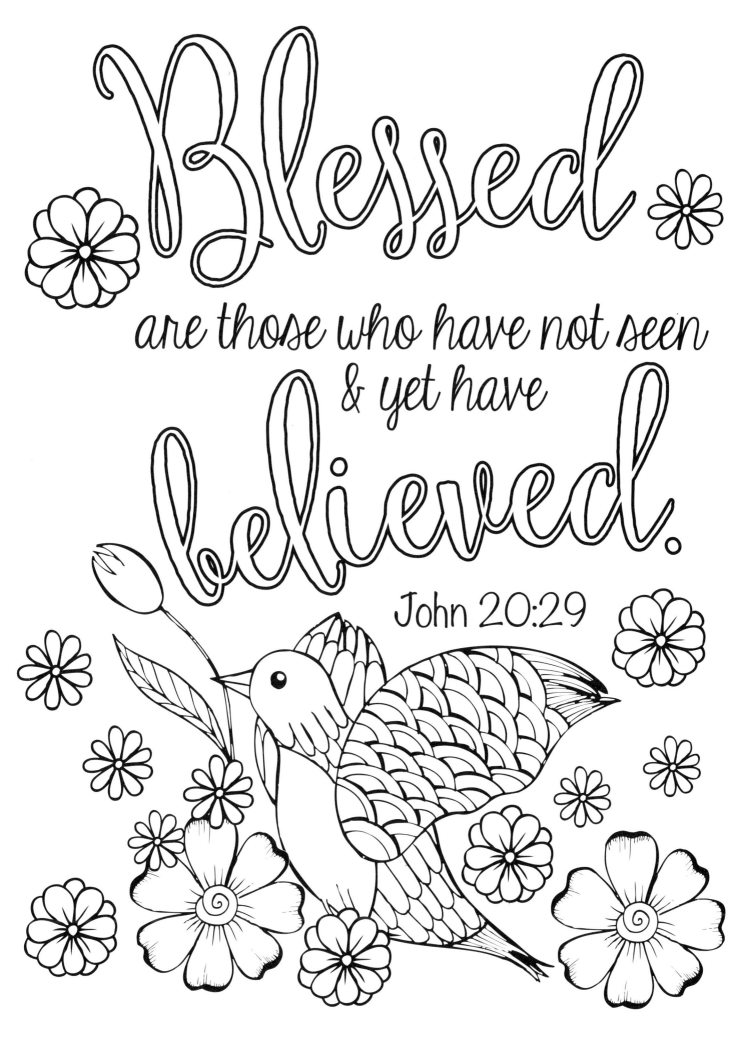

Blessed are those who have not seen & yet have believed.

John 20:29

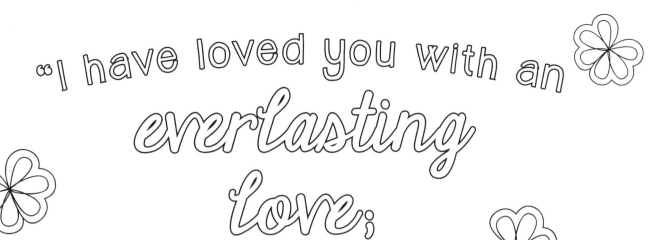

"I have loved you with an *everlasting love;* I have drawn you with unfailing kindness."

Jeremiah 31:3

Whoever believes in the Son has eternal life.

John 3:36

GOD is LOVE

1 John 4:8

Love
the Lord
your
God

with all your
HEART &
with all your soul
with all your STRENGTH.

DEUTERONOMY 6:5

The Lord's delight is in those who put their HOPE IN HIS UNFAILING love.

Psalm 147:11

God's
LOVE & KINDNESS
will shine upon us
like the sun
that RISES
IN THE SKY.

Luke 1:78

My **help** comes from the **LORD,** the **MAKER** of **heaven** & **EARTH!**

Psalm 121:2

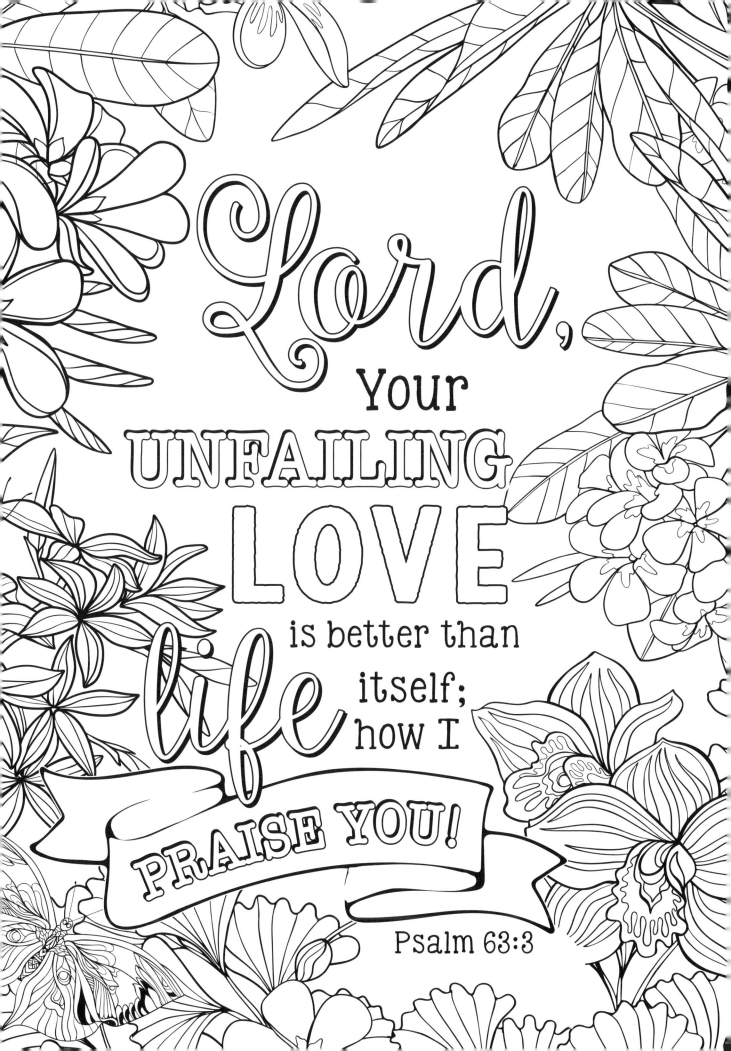

Lord, your UNFAILING LOVE is better than life itself; how I PRAISE YOU!

Psalm 63:3

THE LORD LOVES
RIGHTEOUSNESS
& JUSTICE;
THE EARTH IS FULL OF
HIS UNFAILING
love
PSALM 33:5

As for me,
I will always
have

HOPE

I will praise
You more and
more.

psalm 71:14

YOUR LOVE, Lord, reaches to the HEAVENS, Your faithfulness to THE SKIES.

PSALM 36:5

I wait for the Lord my whole being waits, and in His word I put my hope.

Psalm 130:5

SOW RIGHTEOUSNESS for yourselves, reap the fruit of unfailing love.

Hosea 10:12

No one
who
hopes
IN YOU
will ever be
put to
SHAME.

Psalm 25:3

We LIVE by faith, not by SIGHT.

2 Corinthians 5:7

Faith
comes from hearing,
and hearing through
the word of Christ.

Romans 10:17

Give thanks to the Lord

FOR HE IS GOOD;

HIS LOVE ENDURES FOREVER.

PSALM 118:29

Love

NEVER
FAILS.

1 CORINTHIANS 13:8